Explode The Code

2½

Nancy Hall
Rena Price

Educators Publishing Service
Cambridge and Toronto

Cover by Hugh Price
Text illustrations by Alan Price and Laura Price

Printed in the U.S.A.
ISBN 0-8388-1774-2
978-0-8388-1774-2

10 11 12 13 14 CUR 10 09 08 07 06

CONTENTS

Lesson 1
Read, write, and "X" it.

1. club

   c l u b

2. flip

   _ _ _ _

3. class

   _ _ _ _ _

4. blot

   _ _ _ _

5. glad

   _ _ _ _

6. clam

   _ _ _ _

7. clip

   _ _ _ _

"X" the same word.

1. blob	blab	plop	~~blob~~
2. clad	clap	clad	glad
3. flop	flap	flab	flop
4. glib	glib	glad	glob
5. bliss	gloss	bless	bliss
6. clog	clod	clog	clop
7. glum	slum	glum	plum

2

Match and write it.

| glad | ~~cliff~~ | flag |
| class | flip | clam |

1.

The _c l i f f_ has a flat top.

2.

I can dig for a _____ .

3.

The red _____ flaps.

4.

Sis can do a _____ off the dock.

5.

Glen sits in the _____ .

6.

Pip is _____ he will pass.

◯ it.

bliss (bus) best	fat flat flit
clip cliff crib	clap clip clam
bled glad flag	blot blab club
glass bless gas	flex fix fluff

4

	Spell it.			Write it.
1.	(cl) c	u (i)	zz (ff)	_cliff_
2.	g gl	a e	ss ll	
3.	bl fl	o a	m t	
4.	cl gl	i o	p b	
5.	f fl	a i	ll p	
6.	cl gl	u a	p d	
7.	c cl	a e	m n	

5

Sort the words and write the sentence.

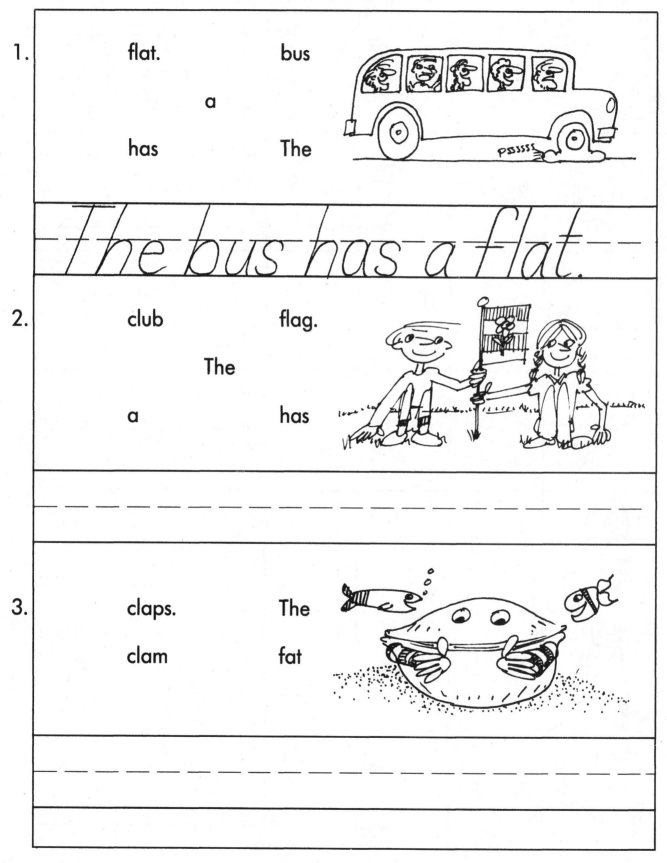

1. flat. bus
   a
   has The

The bus has a flat.

2. club flag.
   The
   a has

3. claps. The
   clam fat

Yes or no?

		No	Yes
1.	Can a pet have fluff?	☐	☒
2.	Will a big flag flap?	☐	☐
3.	Are you glum if you get a flat?	☐	☐
4.	Will a flat clam dig?	☐	☐
5.	Will you clap if you are glad?	☐	☐
6.	Can you do a flip off a cliff?	☐	☐
7.	Are you glad to be in a club?	☐	☐

"X" it.

1.	The cat flips its wig. ☒ The clam flops in the sun. ☐	
2.	The big rug has fluff. ☐ The red pig has a flat top. ☐	
3.	The class claps and claps. ☐ The glass tips a lot. ☐	
4.	Glen fell off the cliff. ☐ Cliff fled from the mad pig. ☐	
5.	Clem is a sad blob. ☐ Clem is glad to win the pin. ☐	
6.	Jan can do a flip. ☐ Jan flips the clip on the can. ☐	
7.	Bess clips her pen to the pad. ☐ Bev puts lip gloss on her lips. ☐	

8

Write it.

1.	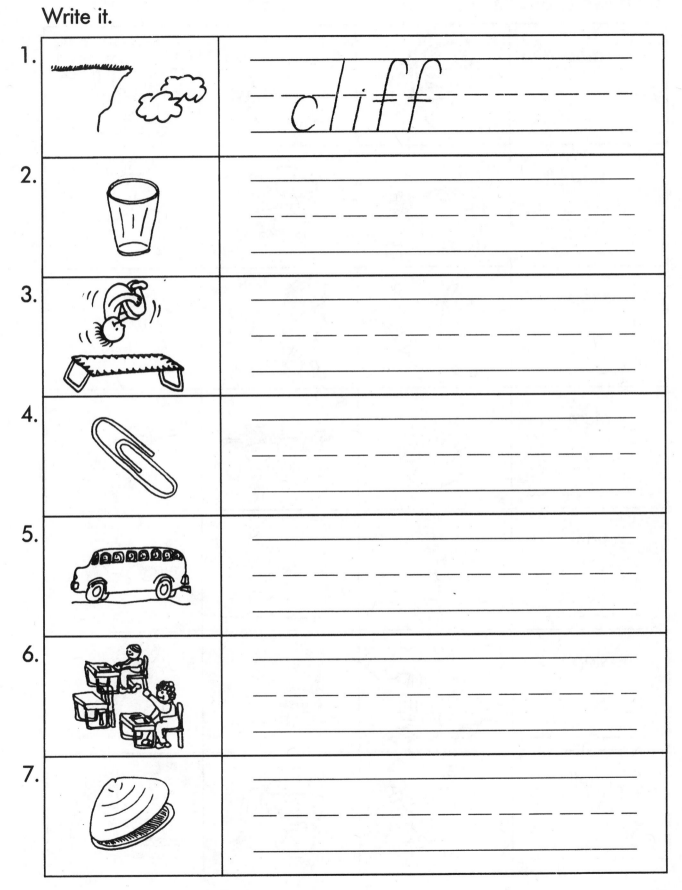	_cliff_
2.		
3.		
4.		
5.		
6.		
7.		

Lesson 2
Read, write, and "X" it.

1.	smog			
	_ _ _ _			

2.	slap			
	_ _ _ _			

3.	snap			
	_ _ _ _			

4.	plum			
	_ _ _ _			

5.	slam			
	_ _ _ _			

6.	slop			
	_ _ _ _			

7.	smell			
	_ _ _ _			

10

"X" the same word.

1.			
plod	plot	plod	blob
2.			
slab	slid	slag	slab
3.			
snit	smut	snit	slit
4.			
snag	snag	smog	snap
5.			
slot	slit	slat	slot
6.			
smog	smug	smog	snug
7.			
snub	snob	snub	shrub

Match and write it.

	plum	slid	plug
	slim	smell	snip

1.   _____

   _ _ _ _ _ _ _ _

Is Mac fat or _____?

2.   _____

   _ _ _ _ _ _ _ _

Will the _____ fit in the slot?

3.   _____

   _ _ _ _ _ _ _ _

You can _____ it in half.

4.   _____

   _ _ _ _ _ _ _ _

Glen can _____ well.

5.   _____

   _ _ _ _ _ _ _ _

The red _____ is big.

6.   _____

   _ _ _ _ _ _ _ _

Wet Dan _____ in the mud.

smog
snob
slob

slum
slim
slam

slam
slap
slim

slid
slap
slug

slit
slap
slid

snap
snip
sniff

plug
plod
glop

slop
slap
slip

13

Spell it.   Write it.

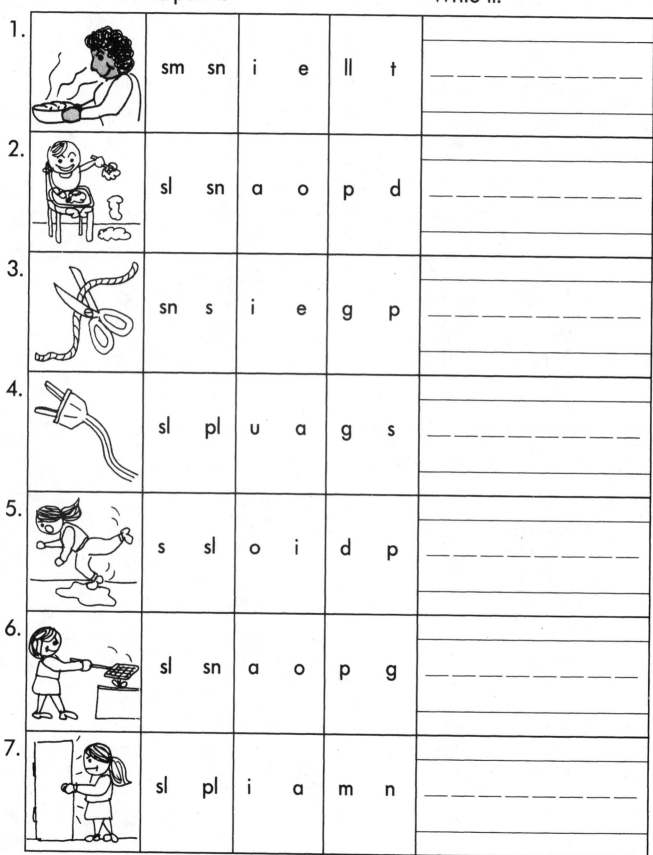

1. sm sn i e ll t   _ _ _ _ _ _ _ _ _ _

2. sl sn a o p d   _ _ _ _ _ _ _ _ _ _

3. sn s i e g p   _ _ _ _ _ _ _ _ _ _

4. sl pl u a g s   _ _ _ _ _ _ _ _ _ _

5. s sl o i d p   _ _ _ _ _ _ _ _ _ _

6. sl sn a o p g   _ _ _ _ _ _ _ _ _ _

7. sl pl i a m n   _ _ _ _ _ _ _ _ _ _

14

Sort the words and write the sentence.

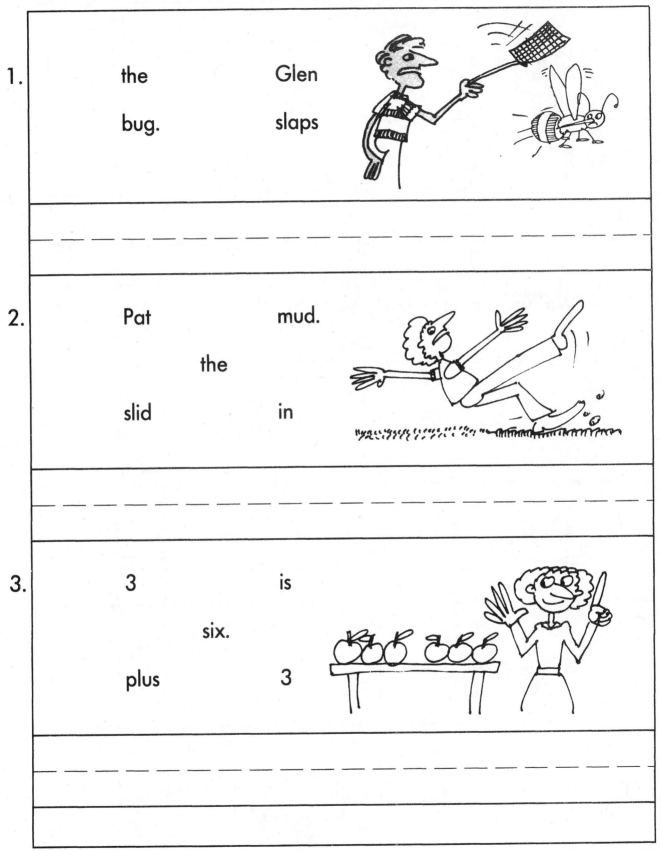

1. the   Glen

   bug.   slaps

_____

2. Pat   mud.

         the

   slid   in

_____

3. 3   is

         six.

   plus   3

_____

Yes or no?

		No	Yes
1.	Can you smell a red plum?	☐	☐
2.	Are you glad if you slam a ball for a run?	☐	☐
3.	Will you snap and zip your bag?	☐	☐
4.	Will Mom be glad if you slap the glass?	☐	☐
5.	Are you sad if you slam the top on your sis?	☐	☐
6.	Is it fun to slip on a wet rug?	☐	☐
7.	Are you glum if your sled slips off the hill?	☐	☐

"X" it.

1.
Bev slugs a run. ☐

Bev hugs a pal. ☐

2.
Clem slits the big box. ☐

The clam sits on the big box. ☐

3.
Deb pulls the plug on Mim. ☐

Mim slips the plug in the slot. ☐

4.
Glen slams the lid on the box. ☐

Jen slams her clog on the bed. ☐

5.
Dot slops pop on the rug. ☐

Dot's pet is a slob. ☐

6.
Biff will get slim if he jogs a lot. ☐

Bill slid in the hog's pen. ☐

7.
Can you smell the hot dog and bun? ☐

The dog sniffs the pot of clams. ☐

Write it.

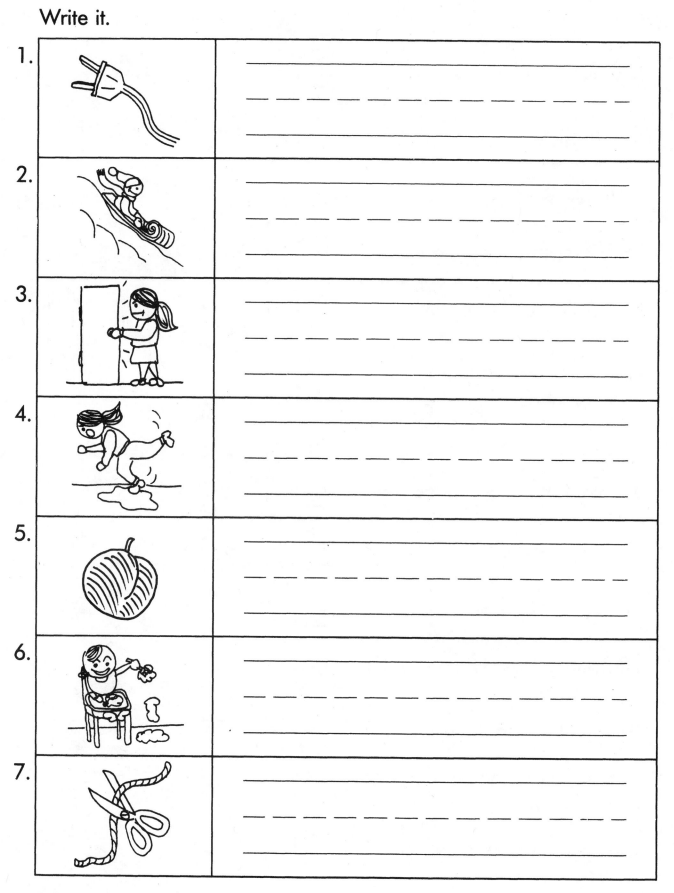

1.

2.

3.

4.

5.

6.

7.

18

Lesson 3
Read, write, and "X" it.

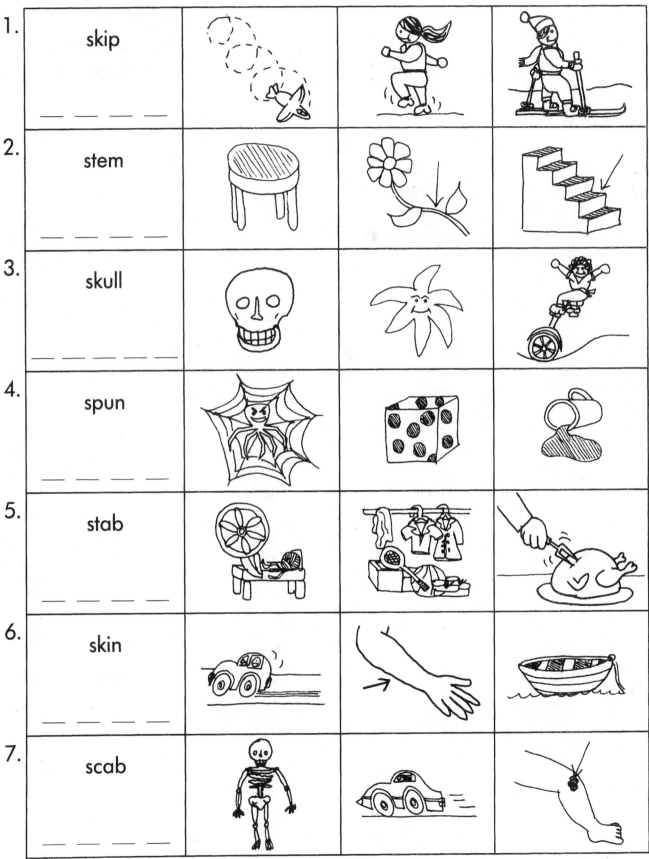

1. skip
   _ _ _ _

2. stem
   _ _ _ _

3. skull
   _ _ _ _ _

4. spun
   _ _ _ _

5. stab
   _ _ _ _

6. skin
   _ _ _ _

7. scab
   _ _ _ _

"X" the same word.

1. scan	scam	scan	cans
2. spud	spat	suds	spud
3. skim	skin	skim	shin
4. still	slit	stiff	still
5. spat	spot	spat	spit
6. stub	stud	stub	stab
7. staff	staff	stuff	stiff

20

Match and write it.

	skin	skid	spell
	scab	steps	spots

1.

_____

_ _ _ _ _ _ _

The fast wet cab will _____ .

2.

_____

_ _ _ _ _ _ _

The _____ is cut off the plum.

3.

_____

_ _ _ _ _ _ _

The big dog has _____ .

4.

_____

_ _ _ _ _ _ _

Ben cannot _____ well.

5.

_____

_ _ _ _ _ _ _

Pam's cut has a _____ on it.

6.

_____

_ _ _ _ _ _ _

Can you skip up the _____ ?

◯ it.

stiff skiff stop	pots spots spits
skill staff stuff	step stop stub
skid kids spin	skull kills skill
spit spill pills	sped spot spud

	Spell it.			Write it.
1.	sp sk	o a	ss ts	_____
2.	s sc	a i	b d	_____
3.	sp st	o u	n m	_____
4.	st sk	e i	d p	_____
5.	s sp	i e	ff ll	_____
6.	st sc	e a	t m	_____
7.	sk s	u i	m n	_____

Sort the words and write the sentence.

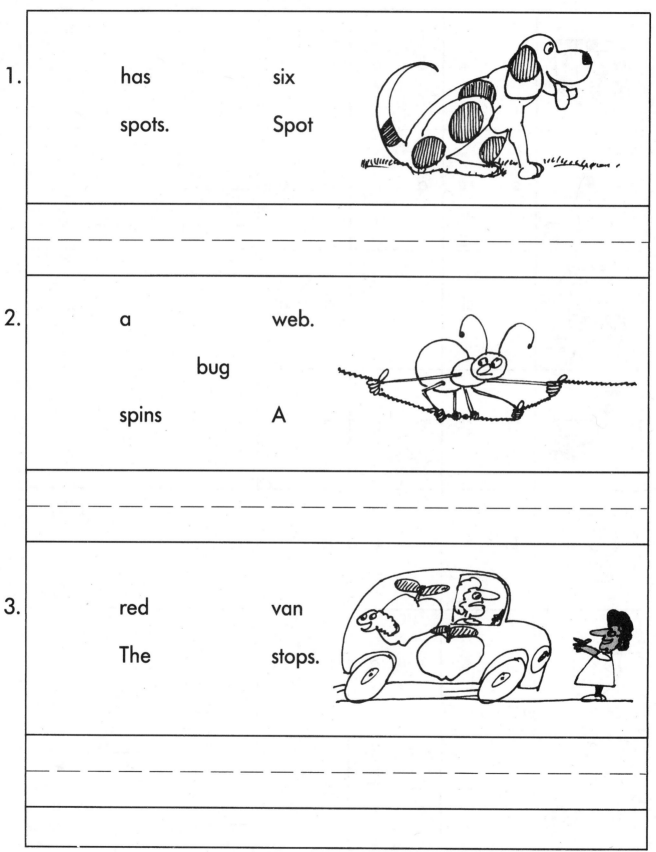

1. has   six

   spots.   Spot

- -

2. a   web.

         bug

   spins   A

- -

3. red   van

   The   stops.

Yes or no?

		No	Yes
1.	Is the stem of a bud stiff?	☐	☐
2.	Can you get wet in a skiff?	☐	☐
3.	Can you stuff your clogs in a bag?	☐	☐
4.	Will a skull have a scab?	☐	☐
5.	Will you step on the flag?	☐	☐
6.	In the hot tub is your skin wet?	☐	☐
7.	Will you stop if you slip on a step?	☐	☐

"X" it.

1.	The stag is as still as can be. ☐ Tad stabs a hot dog. ☐	
2.	The van spins on the steps. ☐ The kid flags the van to stop. ☐	
3.	Scott skips on the steps. ☐ Spot steps on Scott. ☐	
4.	Bev's skin has red spots. ☐ Bev puts on a skit in class. ☐	
5.	Rob spots the flat skiff. ☐ Nell stuffs the doll in the bag. ☐	
6.	Dad spills a glass of pop on Skip. ☐ Skip's dad cuts the grass. ☐	
7.	Len sped past the big bus. ☐ Len stops to let the bus pass. ☐	

Write it.

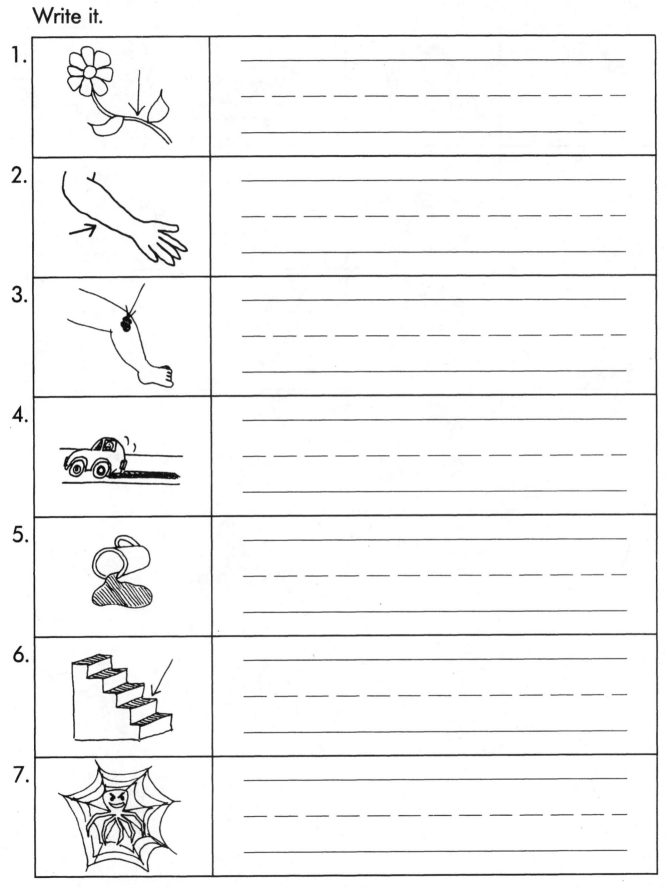

Lesson 4
Read, write, and "X" it.

1. grill
   _ _ _ _ _

2. drum
   _ _ _ _

3. frill
   _ _ _ _ _

4. grin
   _ _ _ _

5. drag
   _ _ _ _

6. crab
   _ _ _ _

7. drop
   _ _ _ _

"X" the same word.

1.	fret	flit	frat	fret
2.	grub	grab	grub	grad
3.	brim	grin	brim	bran
4.	crag	crab	crag	crib
5.	grit	fret	grip	grit
6.	drug	drag	drug	dreg
7.	cram	cram	cran	gram

Match and write it.

grabs   drag   grill

frog   dress   crab

1. Min _____ Al's back.

2. Van can _____ the box.

3. The big _____ grins a lot.

4. Val's _____ has a frill at the neck.

5. The fat _____ sat in the mud.

6. Max flips hot dogs on the _____.

drip
drill
dress

crib
crab
club

grit
grip
prep

cross
dress
press

drab
grab
brag

frog
drug
gruff

grip
prim
drips

crop
crag
crib

	Spell it.			Write it.
1.		dr fr	a o	g d	_ _ _ _ _ _ _ _ _
2.		gr br	i a	ss t	_ _ _ _ _ _ _ _ _
3.		dr gr	a u	d b	_ _ _ _ _ _ _ _ _
4.		dr br	e i	p ll	_ _ _ _ _ _ _ _ _
5.		cr gr	i o	b p	_ _ _ _ _ _ _ _ _
6.		c cr	a u	g b	_ _ _ _ _ _ _ _ _
7.		fr gr	e i	t ll	_ _ _ _ _ _ _ _ _

Sort the words and write the sentence.

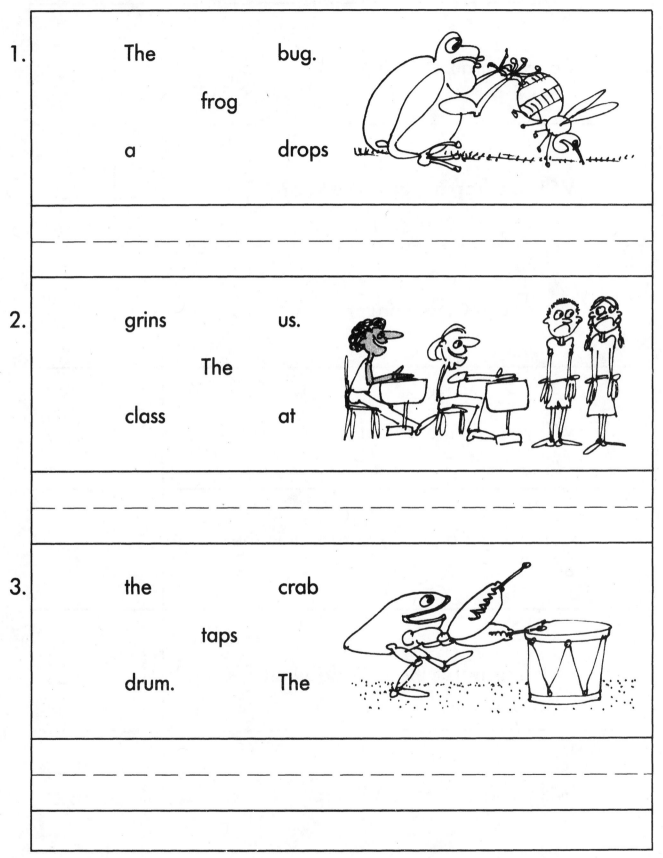

1. The   bug.
           frog
   a   drops

   ----

2. grins   us.
           The
   class   at

   ----

3. the   crab
           taps
   drum.   The

Yes or no?

		No	Yes
1.	Can you grab a frog's leg?	☐	☐
2.	Will you drop a crab in the crib?	☐	☐
3.	Can you grill a big drum?	☐	☐
4.	Will you grin if Brad puts on a dress?	☐	☐
5.	Can you get a pin if you drop it in the grass?	☐	☐
6.	Will you fret if the pop drips on the rug?	☐	☐
7.	Will you grip a drill on its top?	☐	☐

"X" it.

1.
The crab drags a clam to his hill. ☐

The clam drills in the wet mud. ☐

2.
Fred drops his drum in the mud. ☐

The drum drops Fred in the mud. ☐

3.
Deb grabs the hot dog on the grill. ☐

The crab in the pot grins at Deb. ☐

4.
The cross frog clips the grass. ☐

The fat frog has bran and cress in the pan. ☐

5.
The brass bell fell on Brad. ☐

Brad grips the brass bell. ☐

6.
Jen spills hot bran on her dress. ☐

Jen's black dress is drab. ☐

7.
Russ brags a lot to the class. ☐

The class grabs Russ and puts him in a crib. ☐

Write it.

1.

2.

3.

4.

5.

6.

7.

Lesson 5
Read, write, and "X" it.

1.	twig _ _ _ _			
2.	trap _ _ _ _			
3.	press _ _ _ _ _			
4.	twin _ _ _ _			
5.	trot _ _ _ _			
6.	swell _ _ _ _ _			
7.	swam _ _ _ _			

"X" the same word.

1.	prod	prep	prop	prod
2.	tress	truss	trees	tress
3.	swob	swob	swag	swap
4.	twill	twit	trill	twill
5.	trod	trot	trod	trap
6.	swig	swag	wigs	swig
7.	twit	trip	twit	twist

38

Match and write it.

nap	tram	spots
trip	twigs	trots

1. Mag will go on a _____ .

2. The _____ can go to the top.

3. The _____ stick up.

4. Pam has a swell _____ .

5. Dob _____ on the track.

6. Tom _____ a swell dock.

39

○ it.

press **dress** grass	**trip** trap trot
tram **trim** trip	twill twig **twin**
swam swan swig	tram track **trap**
brim **prim** drop	trek tram **trot**

		Spell it.			Write it.
1.		sw sm	i e	m n	_____
2.		t tw	o i	g b	_____
3.		br pr	e a	ff ss	_____
4.		tw sw	u i	n m	_____
5.		dr tr	i a	p m	_____
6.		tr tw	u o	t ck	_____
7.		tw tr	a i	b p	_____

Sort the words and write the sentence.

1.

up   hill.

        Spot

the   trots

2.

Pris

       well.

       swims

3.

at   the   twins

       fox.

grin   The

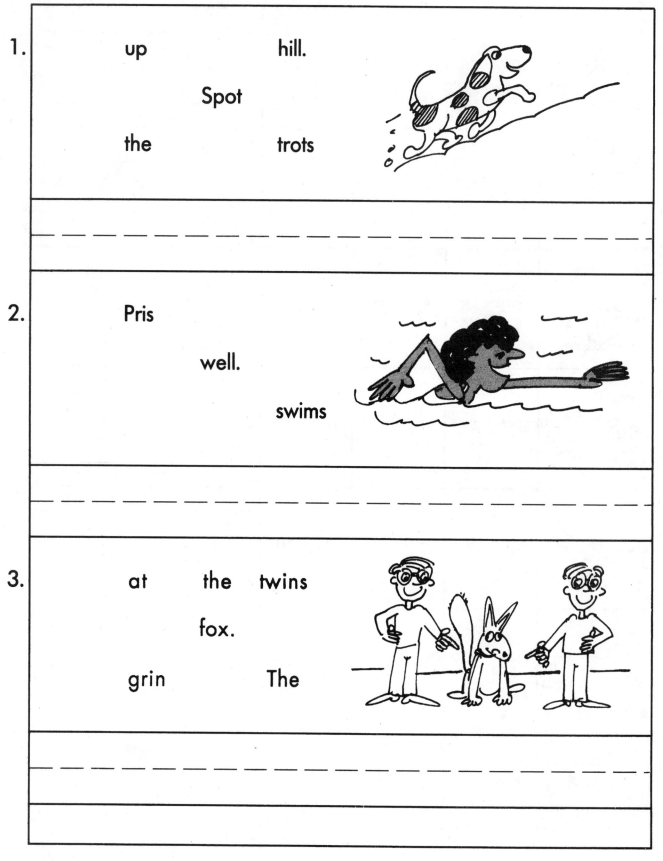

Yes or no?

		No	Yes
1.	Will a tram run off the cliff?	☐	☐
2.	Can you trip on a flat clam?	☐	☐
3.	Is it swell to sit in a hot tub?	☐	☐
4.	Can you trap a crab in a net?	☐	☐
5.	Can you and your Mom be twins?	☐	☐
6.	If you swim a lot, will you be fit and trim?	☐	☐
7.	If you press a plum, will it buzz?	☐	☐

"X" it.

1.	Trip sits on a big crab.	☐	
	Tcm gets a flag on the trip.	☐	
2.	Tess swims a lot and grins.	☐	
	The frog swam up to the trap.	☐	
3.	Buzz trots up the long hill.	☐	
	Buzz grabs the tram on the hill.	☐	
4.	Lin is slim and trim in the red dress.	☐	
	The twins Lin and Slim tap the bell.	☐	
5.	Jen sets a trap for Mom.	☐	
	Dick spots a bill in the grass.	☐	
6.	Dad prods Clem in the back.	☐	
	Clem props the trap up on a twig.	☐	
7.	Pris trips and falls off the dock.	☐	
	Pris is back from a trip.	☐	

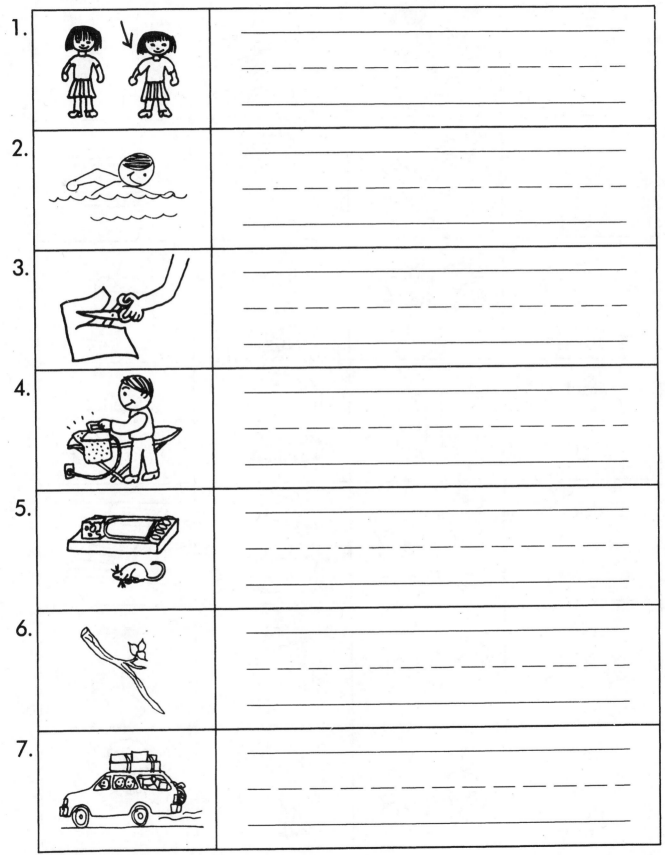

Lesson 6—Final Blends
Read, write, and "X" it.

1. sift
_ _ _ _

2. pants
_ _ _ _ _

3. lift
_ _ _ _

4. tent
_ _ _ _

5. dock
_ _ _ _

6. gift
_ _ _ _

7. ant
_ _ _

46

"X" the same word.

1. luck	tick	luck	lack
2. hint	hunt	tint	hint
3. fact	tack	tact	fact
4. left	felt	lift	left
5. runt	runt	rent	rump
6. tuft	tift	tuft	luff
7. buck	back	duck	buck

Match and write it.

	ant	lock	raft
	act	duck	tent

1. _____

    _ _ _ _ _ _ _ _ _

    Jess will _____ in the skit.

2. _____

    _ _ _ _ _ _ _ _ _

    Jen and Brad sit in the _____ .

3. _____

    _ _ _ _ _

    The brass _____ will fit on the box.

4. _____

    _ _ _ _ _ _ _

    The fat _____ swims well.

5. _____

    _ _ _ _ _

    The _____ is on the hill.

6. _____

    _ _ _ _ _ _ _

    Sam and Ann hid in the _____ .

○ it.

lick luck lock	rent bent hunt
sack sock sick	duck dock deck
gift golf gust	pack peck pass
rats fast raft	act tan ant

Spell it. | Write it.

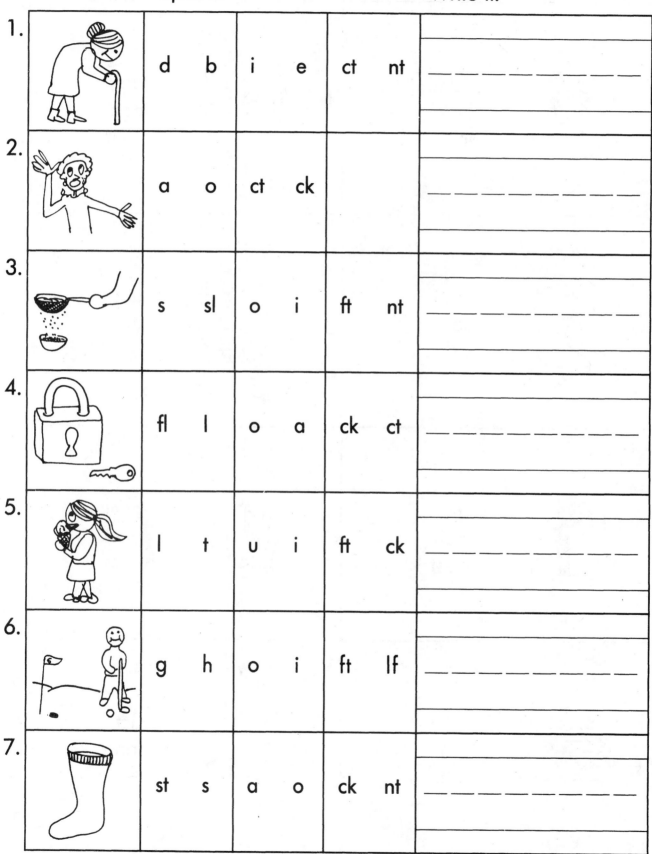

1. | d | b | i | e | ct | nt | _____

2. | a | o | ct | ck | | | _____

3. | s | sl | o | i | ft | nt | _____

4. | fl | l | o | a | ck | ct | _____

5. | l | t | u | i | ft | ck | _____

6. | g | h | o | i | ft | lf | _____

7. | st | s | a | o | ck | nt | _____

Sort the words and write the sentence.

1. socks.   Tim

   his   left

- - - - - - - - - - - - - - - - - - - -

2. the   bent

   Sal   lock.

- - - - - - - - - - - - - - - - - - - -

3. raft.   lifts

   the   Dad

- - - - - - - - - - - - - - - - - - - -

51

Yes or no?

	No	Yes
1. Is a brass lock soft?	☐	☐
2. Can you lift a wet duck?	☐	☐
3. Is it fun to have ants in your socks?	☐	☐
4. If your pup is the runt, is he big and fat?	☐	☐
5. Will you lick a stick of gum?	☐	☐
6. Are you glad if you can swim to the raft?	☐	☐
7. Will a bent twig snap if it is stiff?	☐	☐

"X" it.

1.	Jack picks a spot to set his black bug. ☐ Jack tugs at the bent lock on his pack. ☐		
2.	Pat acts sick as a dog. ☐ The dog picks up the soft sock. ☐		
3.	Rex will hunt for black ducks. ☐ The black ducks tug at the tufts of grass. ☐		
4.	Mick lent Mac a red tent. ☐ Mick drops mint in the glass. ☐		
5.	Kit went to rent a back pack. ☐ Ren packs his pants in a box. ☐		
6.	The last pup is the runt. ☐ Scott rents a swell red raft. ☐		
7.	Gill picks soft fuzz off the duck. ☐ The duck lifts the gift off the dock. ☐		

53

Write it.

1.

2.

3.

4.

5.

6.

7.

Lesson 7
Read, write, and "X" it.

#	Word			
1.	belt — — — —			
2.	lamp — — — —			
3.	film — — — —			
4.	elf — — —			
5.	bulb — — — —			
6.	hump — — — —			
7.	dump — — — —			

"X" the same word.

1.	silk	stilt	silt	silk
2.	self	elfs	self	sulk
3.	damp	bump	dump	damp
4.	wilt	wilt	melt	milk
5.	gulf	gulp	golf	gulf
6.	pulp	pump	pulp	gulp
7.	limp	lump	limb	limp

Match and write it.

| | dump | golf | help |
| | camp | pump | belt |

1. _____

   _ _ _ _ _ _ _ _ _ _ _

   Dan wins at _____ .

2. _____

   _ _ _ _ _ _ _ _

   The _____ can fix a flat.

3. _____

   _ _ _ _ _ _ _ _ _

   Len yells for _____ .

4. _____

   _ _ _ _ _ _ _ _ _ _ _

   Rex has a _____ truck.

5. _____

   _ _ _ _ _ _

   It is fun to have a tent at _____ .

6. _____

   _ _ _ _ _ _ _ _

   Mal has a red _____ .

○ it.

golf
gift
gulp

bump
pump
lamp

hulk
hunt
hump

film
felt
fist

melt
milk
mint

pump
pulp
pups

held
help
hill

silk
self
yelp

Spell it.   Write it.

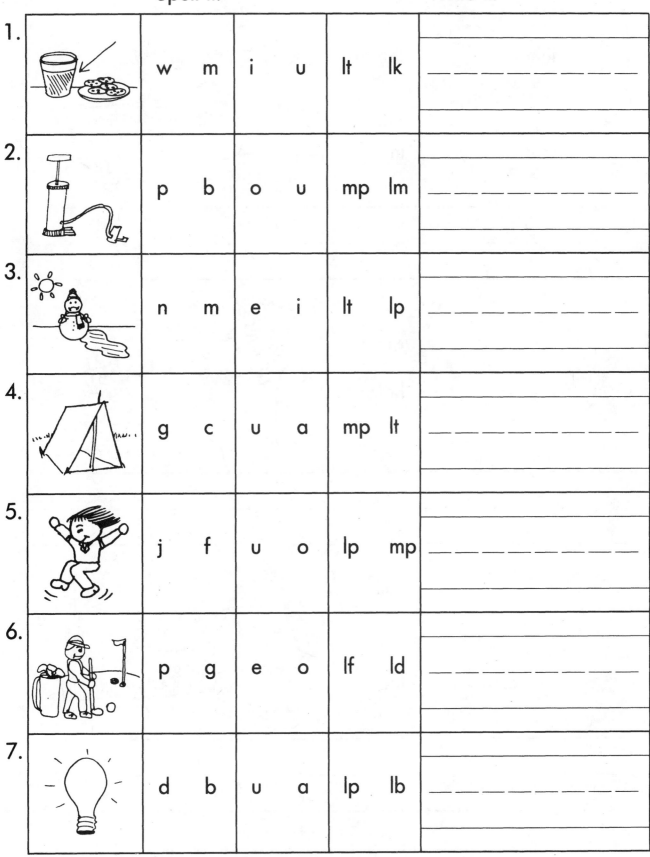

1.	w m	i u	lt lk	_____
2.	p b	o u	mp lm	_____
3.	n m	e i	lt lp	_____
4.	g c	u a	mp lt	_____
5.	j f	u o	lp mp	_____
6.	p g	e o	lf ld	_____
7.	d b	u a	lp lb	_____

Sort the words and write the sentence.

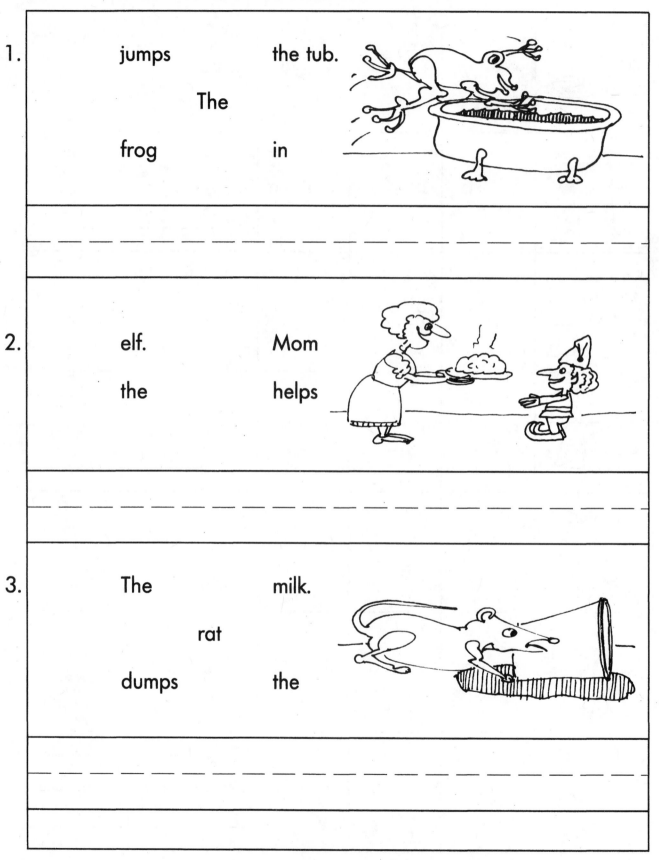

1. jumps   the tub.

       The

  frog   in

- -

2. elf.   Mom

  the   helps

- -

3. The   milk.

     rat

  dumps   the

- -

Yes or no?

		No	Yes
1.	Is it swell to go to camp?	☐	☐
2.	Will you yelp if your snack melts?	☐	☐
3.	Will an elf ask you to go to a film?	☐	☐
4.	Can you get milk from a pump?	☐	☐
5.	Will an elk have a silk belt?	☐	☐
6.	If I'm an imp, will I yell, "Help!" and jump off the raft?	☐	☐
7.	Will you dump Mom's dress in the sink?	☐	☐

"X" it.

1.	The slim crab has a swell belt.	☐	
	The bull held the crab still.	☐	
2.	We have a film of Nat and his golf club.	☐	
	Nat has her fill of golf and snaps her club in half.	☐	
3.	Babs camps in a swell tent.	☐	
	It is swell of Babs to help us fix the ramp.	☐	
4.	The elk has a gulp of milk from the glass.	☐	
	The glass of milk tips and drips on the elf.	☐	
5.	We get damp as we jump off the ramp.	☐	
	It is fun to romp and hunt at the dump.	☐	
6.	Sal helps pump up the raft.	☐	
	Sal held the pump to fix the flat.	☐	
7.	The lamp and bulb help Wes as he hunts for the lock.	☐	
	Ned locks the pump in the snug tent.	☐	

Write it.

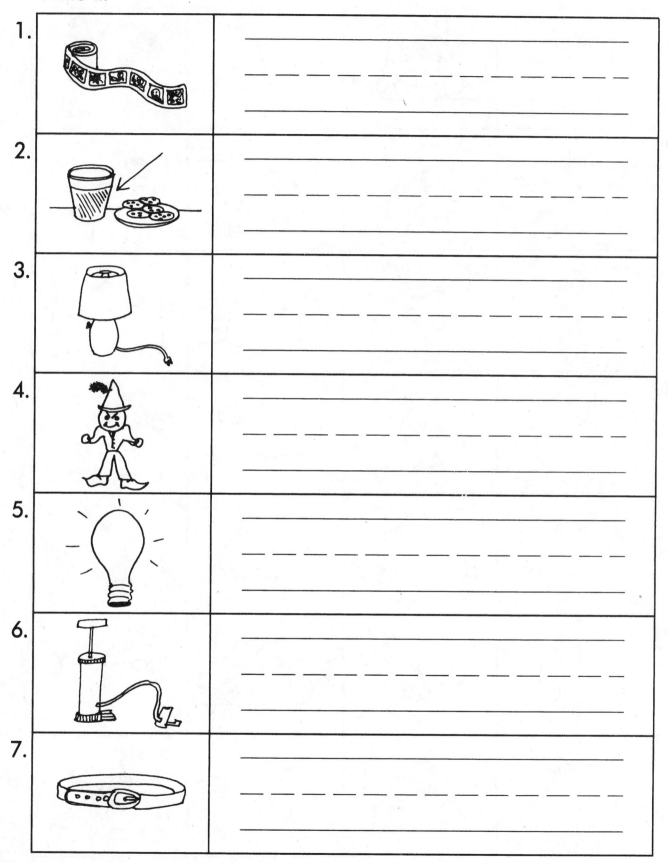

1.

2.

3.

4.

5.

6.

7.

Lesson 8
Read, write, and "X" it.

1.	sand			
	_ _ _ _			
2.	ink			
	_ _ _			
3.	ring			
	_ _ _ _			
4.	bend			
	_ _ _ _			
5.	bunk			
	_ _ _ _			
6.	sang			
	_ _ _ _			
7.	honk			
	_ _ _ _			

64

"X" the same word.

1. bond	dong	band	bond
2. hunk	hunk	hank	hung
3. long	fond	lung	long
4. rung	rang	rung	ring
5. mink	monk	mint	mink
6. land	lend	land	lamb
7. bank	bunk	bank	bang

Match and write it.

ink   rang   sings

winks   wind   pond

1. The pen spills _____ on the desk.

2. Fred _____ a swell song.

3. The big bell _____ and rang.

4. Fran stands in the stiff _____ .

5. The duck swims in the _____ .

6. Cliff _____ at the twins.

junk
jump
just

sing
sink
sent

gong
pond
pods

link
tank
tack

wing
wind
west

wing
wink
wins

sink
sing
silk

bank
bunk
bang

Spell it.   Write it.

1. 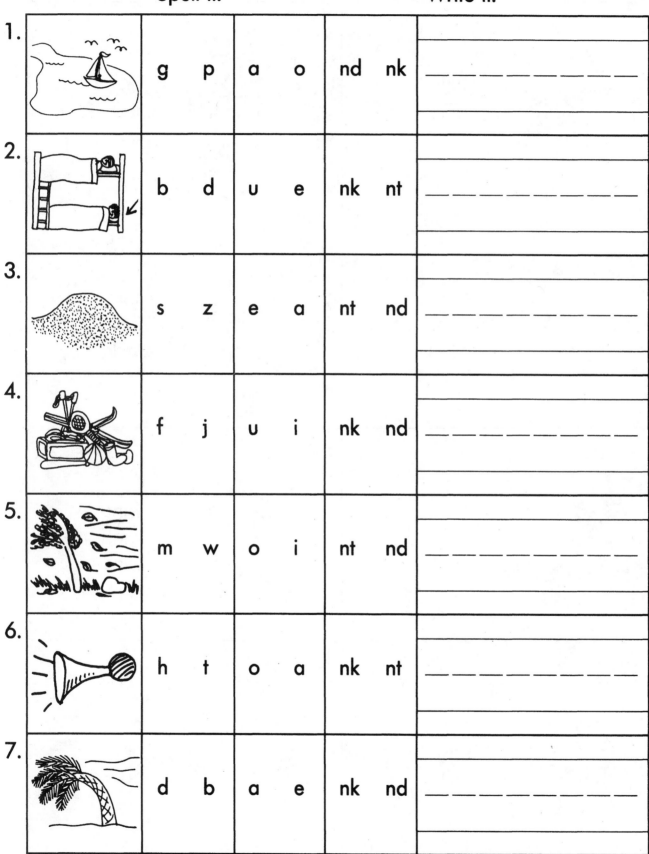	g p	a o	nd nk	_ _ _ _ _ _ _ _ _ _
2.	b d	u e	nk nt	_ _ _ _ _ _ _ _ _ _
3.	s z	e a	nt nd	_ _ _ _ _ _ _ _ _ _
4.	f j	u i	nk nd	_ _ _ _ _ _ _ _ _ _
5.	m w	o i	nt nd	_ _ _ _ _ _ _ _ _ _
6.	h t	o a	nk nt	_ _ _ _ _ _ _ _ _ _
7.	d b	a e	nk nd	_ _ _ _ _ _ _ _ _ _

Sort the words and write the sentence.

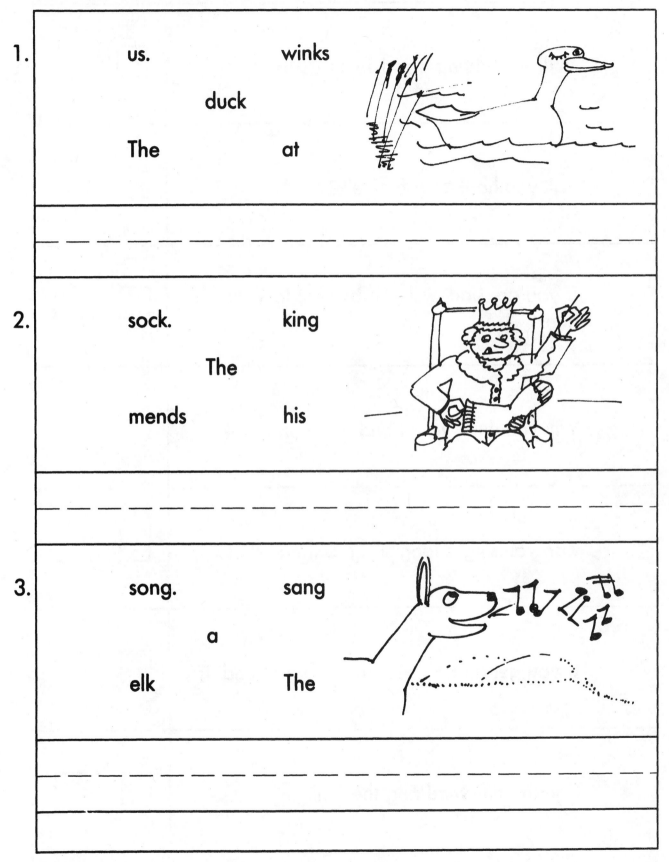

1.

us.   winks

duck

The   at

_____

2.

sock.   king

The

mends   his

_____

3.

song.   sang

a

elk   The

_____

Yes or no?

	No	Yes
1. Will you dump sand in the sink?	☐	☐
2. Will you honk at a pink elk?	☐	☐
3. If you are bad, will you be sent to your bunk?	☐	☐
4. Will you dunk your hand in a can of ink?	☐	☐
5. Can you sing a long song to the end?	☐	☐
6. If you get a ring as a gift, will you bend it?	☐	☐
7. Can the stiff wind ring the bell?	☐	☐

"X" it.

#			
1.	The elk is still on his bunk.	☐	
	The elf skips to the bank.	☐	
2.	The king is fond of the rink.	☐	
	Kim drops her ring in the pond.	☐	
3.	The frog sinks in the pond.	☐	
	Fran sings a song to the band.	☐	
4.	Slim mends his red sock.	☐	
	Slim sends his junk to the dump.	☐	
5.	Ann bends and jogs to be fit.	☐	
	Ann hands the bell to Bud as it rings.	☐	
6.	The duck bent his wing at the rink.	☐	
	Dick winks at the gal in pink silk.	☐	
7.	Liz jumps off the end of the dock.	☐	
	The duck honks at Liz from the pond.	☐	

Write it.

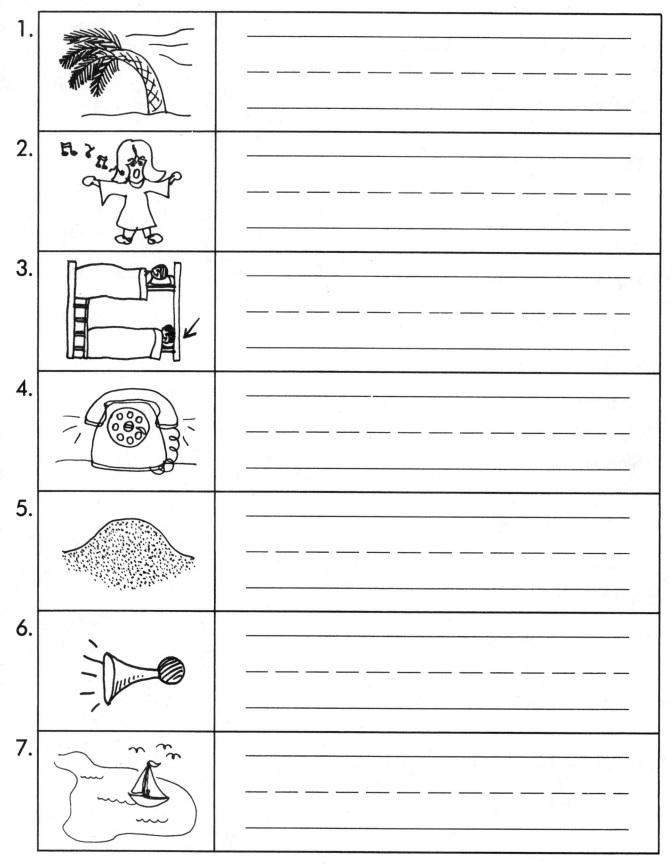

1.

2.

3.

4.

5.

6.

7.

Lesson 9
Read, write, and "X" it.

1.	list ＿ ＿ ＿ ＿			
2.	ask ＿ ＿ ＿			
3.	rest ＿ ＿ ＿ ＿			
4.	tusk ＿ ＿ ＿ ＿			
5.	fast ＿ ＿ ＿ ＿			
6.	risk ＿ ＿ ＿ ＿			
7.	lost ＿ ＿ ＿ ＿			

73

"X" the same word.

1. task	tacks	task	taps
2. wasp	wasp	wisp	wink
3. best	pest	bets	best
4. dusk	ducks	dusk	disk
5. lisp	lips	list	lisp
6. must	west	mist	must
7. pest	pets	pest	past

Match and write it.

	desk tusks cast pest fast asks
1.	_____ _ _ _ _ _ _ _ Tim _____ Sis to lend him her mask.
2.	_____ _ _ _ _ _ _ _ The elf has a _____ on his leg.
3.	_____ _ _ _ _ _ _ _ The gull rests on the _____ .
4.	_____ _ _ _ _ _ _ _ El has a long trunk and _____ .
5.	_____ _ _ _ _ _ _ _ Bets must be a big _____ .
6.	_____ _ _ _ _ _ _ _ The _____ crab slid in the sand.

75

◯ it.

west **vest** rest	nest nets sent
fits **fist** fast	dust ducks **desk**
last lost list	pets step pest
mask mink mast	tusk test vest

		Spell it.			Write it.
1.		d b	a e	ck sk	_____
2.		t l	u a	st sk	_____
3.		t f	u i	sk st	_____
4.		h f	i o	sp st	_____
5.		w m	e a	sk ss	_____
6.		m n	e i	ck st	_____
7.		v w	a e	st sp	_____

Sort the words and write the sentence.

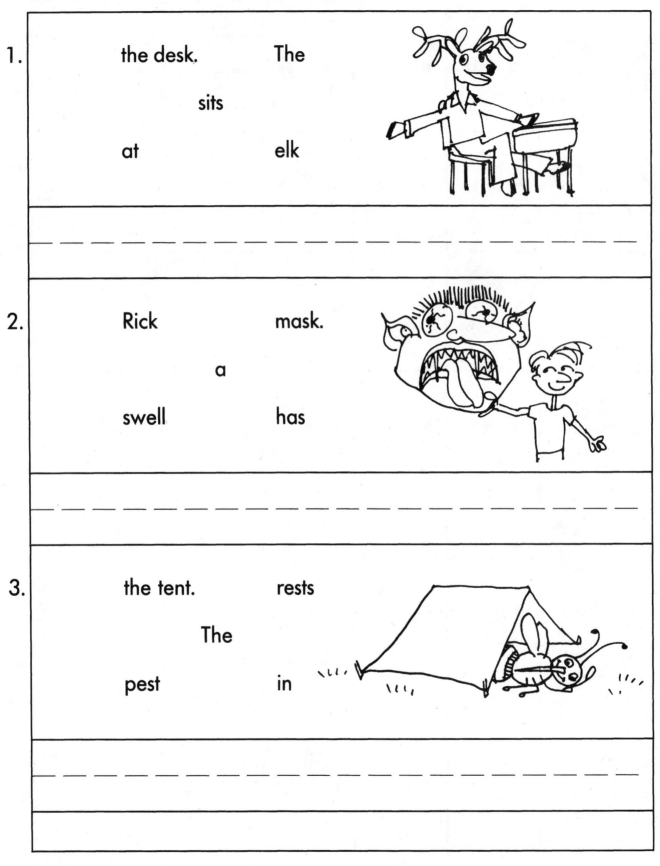

1.
the desk. The

sits

at elk

_ _

2.
Rick mask.

a

swell has

_ _

3.
the tent. rests

The

pest in

_ _

Yes or no?

		No	Yes
1.	Will a king dust his desk?	☐	☐
2.	If you are lost in the mist, will you be sad?	☐	☐
3.	Will an elk have a red vest?	☐	☐
4.	Will you ask a gull if you can rest in its nest?	☐	☐
5.	Will you slam your fist in a wasp's nest?	☐	☐
6.	Will a lock rust if it's damp?	☐	☐
7.	Is it a risk to skid and go fast?	☐	☐

"X" it.

1.	The plump pink ant is a pest. ☐ Pat's pants got wet in the fog. ☐	
2.	Jill must get the long list in the desk. ☐ Fran gets a grand gift from Jill. ☐	
3.	Lost Liz sits on top of the mast. ☐ Rex wept and said he had a big bump. ☐	
4.	Frank has a swig from a big glass. ☐ Tex was the last to swim to land. ☐	
5.	At long last, the big task is at an end. ☐ El has tusks and a swell trunk. ☐	
6.	The pest gets in the desk and dumps the junk. ☐ Pat can't stand the smell of a skunk. ☐	
7.	Pop rests on the drum and has a drink. ☐ Tess held her fist up to slug the pest. ☐	

Write it.

1.

2.

3.

4.

5.

6.

7.

Sometimes a blend can be both at the beginning and the end of a word.

it.

crock clock crack	swept slept swift
blond brand blend	click clock cluck
trust twist tusks	slacks slick slept
track trick truck	craft crock crust

◯ it.

lisp or lips?

stung or stamp?

gasp or grasp?

blest or blast?

elk or end?

drift or draft?

swept or slept?

brick or black?

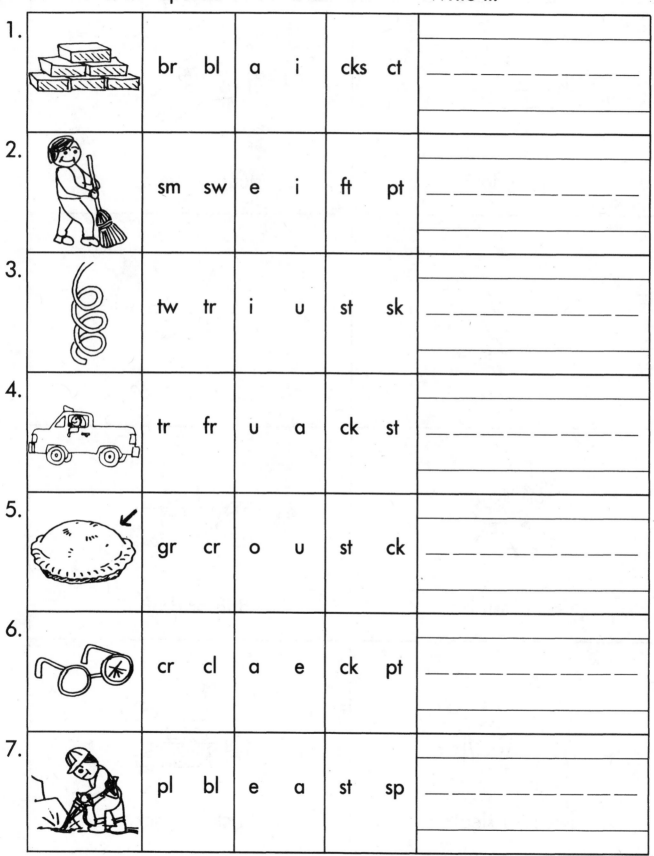

Spell it.   Write it.

1.   br   bl   a   i   cks   ct   _ _ _ _ _ _ _ _ _

2.   sm   sw   e   i   ft   pt   _ _ _ _ _ _ _ _ _

3.   tw   tr   i   u   st   sk   _ _ _ _ _ _ _ _ _

4.   tr   fr   u   a   ck   st   _ _ _ _ _ _ _ _ _

5.   gr   cr   o   u   st   ck   _ _ _ _ _ _ _ _ _

6.   cr   cl   a   e   ck   pt   _ _ _ _ _ _ _ _ _

7.   pl   bl   e   a   st   sp   _ _ _ _ _ _ _ _ _

Match and write it.

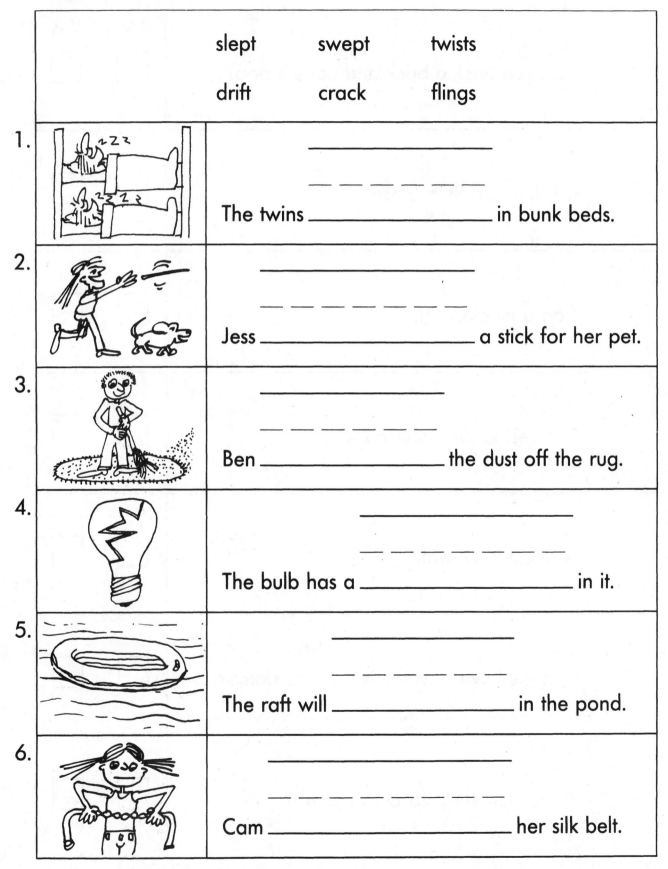

slept   swept   twists

drift   crack   flings

1. The twins _____ in bunk beds.

2. Jess _____ a stick for her pet.

3. Ben _____ the dust off the rug.

4. The bulb has a _____ in it.

5. The raft will _____ in the pond.

6. Cam _____ her silk belt.

Yes or no?

		No	Yes
1.	Can you prick a brick and have it pop?	☐	☐
2.	Is it fun to drift in a raft?	☐	☐
3.	Can a jet blast off?	☐	☐
4.	Is it best to lock your desk?	☐	☐
5.	Is a fast truck swift?	☐	☐
6.	Can we have frost if it is hot and damp?	☐	☐
7.	Have you slept in a top bunk?	☐	☐

"X" it.

1.	The frog slept in the duck's nest. ☐ The frog swept the duck's nest. ☐		
2.	Wes gets his best slacks wet at the pond. ☐ The flat steps are slick if they are wet. ☐		
3.	The ants have a blast at the rink. ☐ Ann lost her best ring at the rink. ☐		
4.	The hens cluck and pick at the soft crusts. ☐ Clem twists the bell off as the clock rings six. ☐		
5.	The swift truck skids on a wet spot. ☐ Lost Sal trusts the elf to help her get to the West. ☐		
6.	The blond blasts off in a long jet. ☐ Jen plucks quills from her blond dog. ☐		
7.	Matt bends and twists his neck to spot the track. ☐ Matt bends to lift the last block and twists his back. ☐		

Write it.

1.

2.

3.

4.

5.

6.

7.

◯ it.

	bland blend brand		trick trunk tank
	plank prick prank		twist twins twigs
	blend spend spunk		blink drink blank
	spank slink skunk		stand sand trend

$\bigcirc$ it.

stink or slink?

flunk or flack?

blank or blink?

plank or plan?

blend or blank?

wept or swept?

bond or blond?

prank or plant?

Spell it.   Write it.

1.		st	sw	a	e	nk	pt
2.		tr	br	u	a	ck	nk
3.		pl	bl	e	o	ng	nd
4.		sp	st	i	a	nk	nd
5.		sl	sp	e	i	nd	mp
6.		sp	sk	o	u	ng	nk
7.		pl	fr	u	a	nk	nd

Match and write it.

stands   drinks   grand

plank   stink   flunks

1. Frank _____ on his desk and sings.

2. Min's gift was _____ .

3. Bets _____ the test.

4. Clem has a long _____ for a ramp.

5. El _____ a big glass of milk.

6. A skunk can _____ .

Yes or no?

		No	Yes
1.	Can you drink a glass of mist?	☐	☐
2.	Can a blond duck cluck?	☐	☐
3.	Are you a crank if you yell and act mad?	☐	☐
4.	Will you spank a skunk if it stinks?	☐	☐
5.	Are you at your best if you flunk a test?	☐	☐
6.	Will you stand still for a prank?	☐	☐
7.	Do you have tusks and a long trunk?	☐	☐

"X" it.

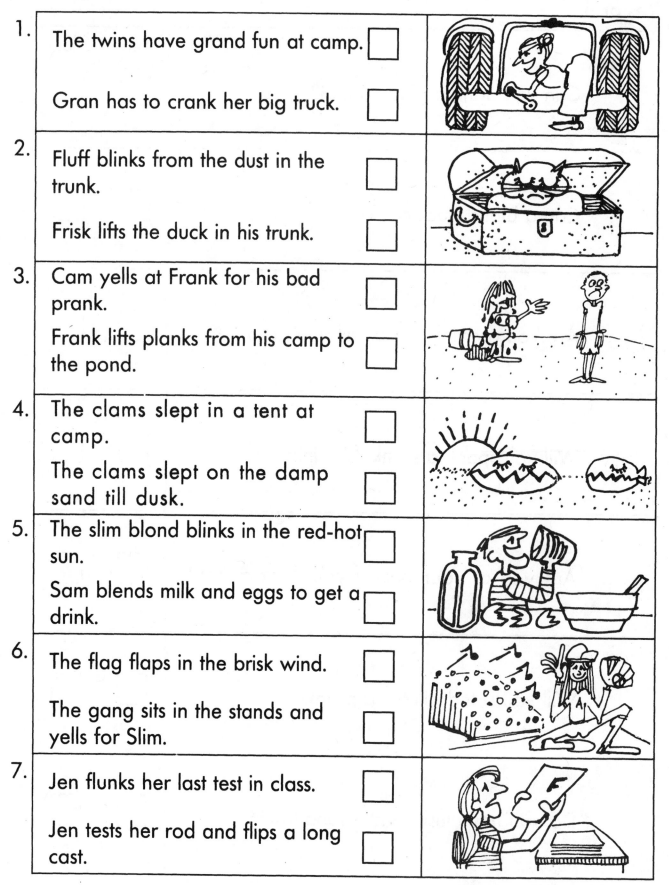

1. The twins have grand fun at camp. ☐

   Gran has to crank her big truck. ☐

2. Fluff blinks from the dust in the trunk. ☐

   Frisk lifts the duck in his trunk. ☐

3. Cam yells at Frank for his bad prank. ☐

   Frank lifts planks from his camp to the pond. ☐

4. The clams slept in a tent at camp. ☐

   The clams slept on the damp sand till dusk. ☐

5. The slim blond blinks in the red-hot sun. ☐

   Sam blends milk and eggs to get a drink. ☐

6. The flag flaps in the brisk wind. ☐

   The gang sits in the stands and yells for Slim. ☐

7. Jen flunks her last test in class. ☐

   Jen tests her rod and flips a long cast. ☐

94

Write it.

1.

2.

3.

4.

5.

6.

7.

Lesson 12—Final Review

◯ it.

slant stint stunt	skimp stamp stump
stack slacks smacks	sting sing sling
slant stamp slump	spin spent spunk
print plank plant	sting sling swing

96

plank or pack?

flint or fling?

truck or trunk?

plant or grant?

drank or plank?

grasp or crust?

slant or slump?

trust or twist?

Spell it.   Write it.

1. 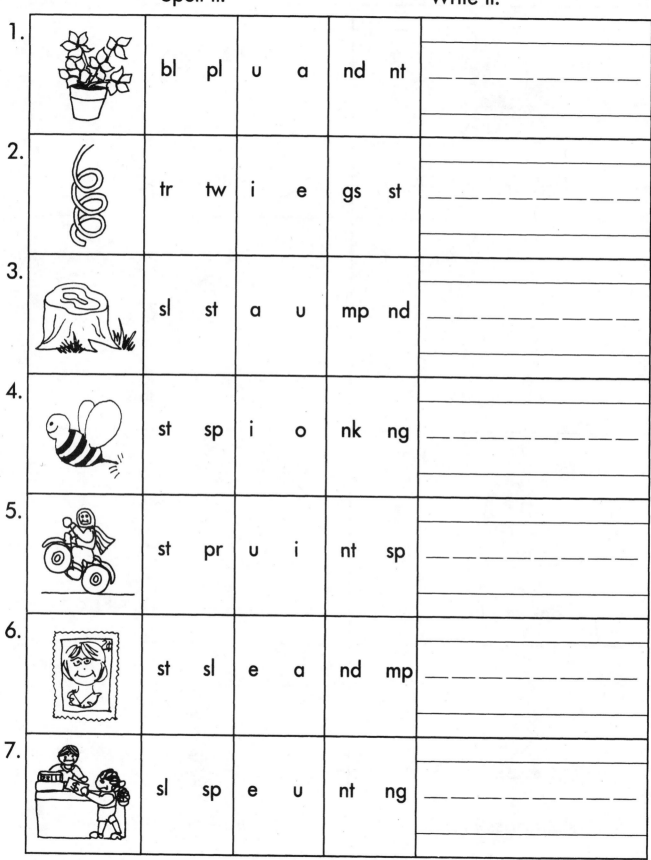	bl pl	u a	nd nt	_____
2.	tr tw	i e	gs st	_____
3.	sl st	a u	mp nd	_____
4.	st sp	i o	nk ng	_____
5.	st pr	u i	nt sp	_____
6.	st sl	e a	nd mp	_____
7.	sl sp	e u	nt ng	_____

Match and write it.

| | swing | plant | stump |
| | flings | grasps | stung |

1. Grant twists in the _____ _____ .

2. Pris _____ _____ the stick for Stub.

3. Gramp will _____ _____ the grass.

4. Clem sits on a _____ _____ and drinks.

5. Bell got _____ _____ on her leg.

6. Tom _____ _____ the mast so he can't slip.

Yes or no?

		No	Yes
1.	Can you swing a golf club at a plant?	☐	☐
2.	Can you do a stunt on a swing?	☐	☐
3.	If you are plump, are you thin?	☐	☐
4.	Will you grunt if you tug on a stump?	☐	☐
5.	Can you grasp a flag in your hand?	☐	☐
6.	If you are stung, will you swell?	☐	☐
7.	Are you fond of crisp crust?	☐	☐

"X" it.

1.	Gramp is plump and lots of fun. ☐ Gramp is sick and must rest. ☐	
2.	Brant brings Babs a plump frog. ☐ Brant prints "Babs" on his hand. ☐	
3.	Floss has her front leg in a sling. ☐ Floss flings her blond wig at Slim. ☐	
4.	Grant puts a pink plant on his desk. ☐ Grant brings planks for the long dock. ☐	
5.	Flip grabs Lin's mask and twists it. ☐ Flip grasps Lin's hand and helps her. ☐	
6.	Pol plans to do a stunt for the class. ☐ Pol is a scamp and puts wax on the swing. ☐	
7.	Frank drifts in the craft. ☐ Frank is stung and yells for help. ☐	

Write it.

1.

2.

3.

4.

5.

6.

7.

1. blend bland blind blond	2. skip scant scamp skimp
3. slum slant slump slung	4. blast draft drift drank
5. blank bland blink brand	6. clung clump clamp clank
7. twist trust truck tusk	8. crust crest clasp crisp

(Teacher dictated. See Key for Book 2½.)

1.

2.

3.

4.

5.

6.

Write the word.

1.

It is fun. You have a ball and ten clubs. You swing a club in your hand and send the ball to the cup. But if you do not slam it, the ball will end in the pond. _G_____ is lots of fun.

2.

It is big and can rust. It can help you a lot. You can put your junk on it and go to the dump. You can put a top on it and go on a trip. It can skid or get stuck in the mud. It can go fast and honk its horn. It is a _t_____ .

3.

You can swim and jump off the raft. You can do crafts and sing songs. You will get bunks in a tent. It is grand fun to go to _C_____ .

4.

It swims next to the rocks and grass. It is swift. If you have a net on a long stick, you can get it. You flip your net and twist it fast so it will not swim off. If you pick it up, it must be held on the back of its shell, not the front, or you will yelp. It is a _C_____ .

Match and write it.

> trunk   pranks   song   plant
>
> clasp   winks   plump   drink

1. _____

A pink _____ smells swell.

2. _____

Sal sings a _____ and hits a drum.

3. _____

Slim grins and _____ at Floss.

4. _____

I will _____ a big glass of milk.

5. _____

Dad tells Will to stop his bad _____.

6. _____

Jill packs slacks and socks in a big _____.